CONTEMPORARY BRITISH
MEDALS

D1242517

CONTEMPORARY BRITISH
MEDALS

MARK JONES

Published for the
Trustees of the British Museum by
British Museum Publications

© 1986 Trustees of the British Museum
Published by British Museum Publications Limited
46 Bloomsbury Street, London WC1B 3QQ

British Library Cataloguing in Publication Data

Jones, Mark
    Contemporary British medals.
    1. Medals—Great Britain—Exhibitions
    I. Title
    737'.22'0941074   CJ6102

ISBN 0-7141-0864-2

Front and back cover subject: Lynn Chadwick *Diamond* cat. no. 1

Designed by Harry Green
Set in Linotron 202 Palatino
and printed in Great Britain by
Hazell Watson & Viney Limited

The Trustees of the British Museum
acknowledge with gratitude the support of

Silich-von Schulthess AG
Investment Advisors and Trustees

and

Bank Leu Ltd
Numismatics

in the publication of this book.

Photography by
David Webb, Charles Howson and Brian McCarthy

Opposite Elisabeth Frink *Peace Medal* 1977 (cat. no. 2)

Contents

Fred Kormis *John Schlesinger* 1983
(cat. no. 4)

Preface

Collecting and exhibiting contemporary medals is not a new activity for the British Museum. The founding collection, in the mid-eighteenth century, contained a number of recently produced pieces which were exhibited, along with manuscripts and antiquities, in the rooms of Montagu House. The acquisition of new medals, both British and foreign, continued through the late-eighteenth and nineteenth centuries. In our own century a substantial collection of German Expressionist medals was formed during and after the First World War and placed on exhibition in the 1920s.

In more recent years, however, attention has moved from the acquisition of contemporary work to the collecting of earlier medals and it was not until the late-seventies that the former tradition was resumed. Indeed, the Museum's interest in this material may have influenced a revival in the art of the medallist in Britain. Almost all the pieces included in this catalogue have entered the Museum's collection since that time, either by purchase or due to the generosity of the artists concerned. The result is seen in this travelling exhibition which will, we hope, introduce a wider public to a varied and exciting range of recent medallic work, much of which is shown here for the first time.

Medals are relatively cheap and small and provide an opportunity for the collector of moderate means to acquire works by leading sculptors, and as such can be compared to the artist's original print; it is therefore hoped that this exhibition will stimulate a field of artistic patronage which has long lain fallow.

D M WILSON
Director of the British Museum

Introduction

The last fifteen years have seen a marked revival of interest in the medal among a surprising range of British artists. Sculptors, working in a variety of idioms and media, jewellers and poets, engravers and cartoonists, painters and silversmiths, have all found something of interest in the medallic tradition and have brought new ideas and original contributions to that tradition. It is the purpose of this exhibition, in gathering these new contributions, to convey the energy that led to their creation and to show the dynamic effect that they have had on this, least known of the arts.

Talk of a revival should not be thought to imply a golden past, for the history of medallic art in Britain is neither glorious nor unbroken. Native to northern Italy and thriving in much of central and southern Europe by

Nicholas Hilliard
Dangers Averted 1589

the early sixteenth century, the medal was a tardy and somewhat sickly addition to British culture. Nicholas Hilliard's medals of Queen Elizabeth, though glamorous and brilliantly executed, were isolated and overshadowed by the popularity of his own and others' portrait miniatures. The Simons, Thomas and Abraham, were among the most distinguished portraitists of the Commonwealth, but after Thomas' effective replacement by the Belgian Roettiers family under Charles II, it was to be over a hundred and fifty years before the Wyons were to make the next major British contribution to the history of the medal, in the nineteenth century. The twentieth century has, at least until recently, been if anything less remarkable than the eighteenth.

The lack of native talent revealed by this brief historical survey has been a source of intermittent concern since at least the early seventeenth century. Charles I, dismayed by the 'imperfection and disequalities' that he noted in British coins, employed a Frenchman, Nicolas Briot, to 'provide a new portrait for the coinage and to make medals of all sorts . . . which might convey to posterity the mark and character of worthy success, accidents or great actions'. Charles II, as we have seen, imported Jan Roettiers and two of his sons while, after the Glorious Revolution and the consequent defection of these Catholic engravers, successive sovereigns were ably served by the German Johann Croker.

Shortly after Croker's death in the mid-eighteenth century Henry Baker,

9

seriously concerned at the state of medallic art in Britain, engaged the newly founded Society of Arts, Manufacturers and Commerce in an effort to improve the situation by offering an annual prize for the copper medal which 'shall be executed the best in point of workmanship and boldness of relief.' This prize lapsed in 1765 but was revived in the early nineteenth century. Shortly before this Wellesley Pole, then Master of the Mint, turned to an Italian, Benedetto Pistrucci, in an attempt to improve the lamentable standard of coin and medal design, an attempt which bore fruit both in Pistrucci's beautiful *St George and the Dragon* design for the coinage and in the public interest and esteem which his later unpopularity won for his talented English rival William Wyon. The vacuum left by William Wyon's death in 1851 had once again to be filled by a consciously planned effort at renewal, conceived by Reginald Stuart Poole (Keeper of Coins and Medals at the British Museum), headed by Charles Fremantle (Deputy Master of the Royal Mint) and including on its committee a number of well-known contemporary artists such as Leighton, Boehm, Thornycroft, Poynter and Alma-Tadema, Leonard Wyon and Alphonse Legros. The last of these was to prove the most effective member of the Society. As Slade Professor at University College London, he fostered a whole generation of younger

Alphonse Legros
Alfred Tennyson 1881. 120 mm

artists for whom medals were a natural medium, including Feodora Gleichen, Elinor Hallé, William Rothenstein and Charles Holroyd. However despite Legros' efforts, and those of his friend Edouard Lanteri, and despite the fine work produced by sculptors like William Goscombe John and Gilbert Bayes in the early twentieth century, no successor-generation emerged. Indeed by the mid-twentieth century Paul Vincze and F. J. Kormis, both born and trained in Central Europe, were almost the only committed proponents of medallic art in Britain.

Given this history it can come as no surprise that the recent revival of interest in the medal had its origin in institutional patronage, emanating

Jacqueline Stieger
Harrogate Festival 1975
Commissioned by the Goldsmith's Company (cat. no. 2)

from three major bodies, each working independently to introduce a new generation to medallic art in the mid 1970s.

First of the three was the Goldsmiths' Company, whose then Director of Art, Graham Hughes, organised *Medals Today* in 1973. This was the first major exhibition of contemporary medals to be held in Britain since 1956 (when Humphrey Sutherland organised the exhibition at the Royal Society of Arts which initially sparked Graham Hughes' interest in the subject).

This showed a representative sample of European medals alongside a comprehensive selection of British work, much of which had been commissioned especially for the exhibition. Included were works by Malcolm Appleby, Jocelyn and Michael Burton, Geoffrey Clarke, Leslie Durbin, Ian Godfrey, Patrick Hughes, Louis Osman, John Piper and Jacqueline Stieger, most of whom were experimenting with medallic work for the first time.

In his other role, as Head of Design at the Royal Mint, Graham Hughes, with the backing of the then Deputy Master, Harold Glover, reintroduced the practice of splash striking medals from hand engraved dies (Malcolm Appleby's *Birds of Destiny* and *Human Butterfly* were two early examples). He also, particularly in connection with the later *Loot* exhibitions, commissioned medals from Malcolm Appleby and Martin Page which demonstrated that pieces of considerable quality could be struck and sold at prices that confronted the cheap 'souvenir' medal head on.

It was the Royal Mint, in collaboration with the Money and Medals Programme of the Food and Agriculture Organisation under Raymond Lloyd, which acted as a second new patron of the medal. Commissions for the FAOS CERES medals went to a number of British artists including both artists already known for their medallic work like Jacqueline Stieger, Geoffrey

James Butler
Iris Murdoch 1975 (cat. no. 1)

Clarke and David Wynne and those for whom medals were a new departure, like James Butler, Ivor Roberts-Jones and Vivien ap Rhys-Pryce. More recently, under Clive Stannard, the FAO organised a competition for their World Food Day medal which was won by Frank Forster.

Both the Goldsmiths and the Royal Mint/FAO were working to introduce a wider range of already established artists to medallic art. The need to nurture a new generation of medallists was recognised by Peter Seaby (of

Jane McAdam
Picasso 1980 (cat. no. 1)

the firm of coin and medal dealers B. A. Seaby Ltd) who approached the Royal Society of Arts and persuaded it to revive its earlier role as patron of the medal by offering to fund a medal section in the annual design bursary competition. With the assistance of the Royal Mint casting unit this began to attract students from an ever widening range of Art Colleges and, over the years, has introduced a whole new generation, including Mark Holloway, Jane McAdam, Fred Rich, Cecilia Leete, Lloyd Carter and Gillian Colver, to the potential of medallic art. The medal bursary competition also attracted as sponsors not only public or charitable bodies like the British Museum and the Goldsmiths' Company but also a number of the private companies making and issuing medals, such as the Birmingham, Pobjoy and Tower Mints and Spink and Sons. This second category is of particular importance because it is companies like these who have the most direct influence on the standard of medal design and the strongest long term interest in forming a new and talented generation of medallists.

Though what we have seen so far mirrors, and in the case of the RSA repeats, the pattern of earlier patronage, one element, previously provided by the Society of Medallists, was missing. With the backing of Helen Auty

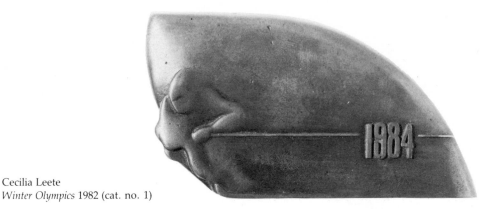

Cecilia Leete
Winter Olympics 1982 (cat. no. 1)

at the RSA and the financial support of the Goldsmiths this gap was filled by the foundation of the British Art Medal Society in Spring 1982. This new society at once began to commission medals, both from existing medallists like Ron Dutton, Jacqueline Stieger, Michael Rizzello and Malcolm Appleby and from sculptors like Nigel Hall, John Maine, Lynn Chadwick and Paul Neagu who had not previously made medals. The Art Medal Society, however, worked not only to provide a stimulus to artists, but also to provide a larger and better informed public for their work through its magazine *The Medal* and through conferences, lectures and exhibitions.

All of this may be taken to suggest that medallic art is, and always has been, something of a forced growth in Britain. But it would not be fair to conclude that the recent revival of interest in medals has been entirely, or even largely, the result of a calculated campaign by a few institutional patrons. It could be argued with equal force that this patronage was itself a reaction to the outstanding work produced privately and spontaneously by a number of contemporary artists.

Ron Dutton with his sustained and dedicated search for a medallic expression of his personal response to landscape; Ian Hamilton Finlay, the great Scottish poet and gardener, with his telling meditations on the relation between images of modern warfare and the work of Dante, Beethoven and Heraclitus; Geoffrey Clarke in his extensive exploration of man's conflict with the environment and Robert Elderton in his highly personal yet popularly accessible portraits are among those who have aroused the enthusiasm which the unparalleled level of patronage seen in recent years reflects.

This patronage has come, not just from the committed institutions discussed above but also from individuals, who commission birthday, wedding, anniversary, retirement and memorial medals and from a range of universities, colleges, societies, companies and local authorities. Recent patrons include the Society of Education Officers (Schools Curriculum Award Medals by Fred Rich, Jane McAdam and Cecilia Leete), Liverpool University, Hull School of Architecture and the Arms and Armour Society (Jacqueline Stieger), Sothebys and the Wellcome Foundation (Fred Rich), the Fabian Society, the Victorian Society, the West Midland Physicians, the Phytochemical Society of Europe and the Historical Association (Ron Dutton) and Morgan Grenfell (Jane McAdam). The reasons for this revival of interest must be sought neither in the prestige conferred upon the patron nor in the profitable opportunities offered to the artist, for both were negligible, but in the particular characteristics of the medal. Medals are, by custom, lim-

ited in size, shape, material and function. They are small, round, metal and two sided; they bear images in low relief (a portrait on one side and an allegory on the other) and inscriptions; their function is to portray, to commemorate and to reward; and they are made to be multiplied (the intentionally unique medallic work is almost a contradiction in terms). This is not to suggest either that there has ever been a period in which every medal conformed to the ideal or that medallic art has remained untouched by the developments of the last century. Naturally it has responded to developments in both the fine and decorative arts, so that we have seen both the art nouveau medal and the medal as impression, the art deco medal and the medal as abstraction, the medal as *objet trouvé*, assemblage, record of gesture and process, the serial medal and the anti medal. But even so it has remained, both in the public mind and in the work of the majority of its practitioners, a conservative and traditional medium.

Sometimes, indeed, the medal seems stranded in the distant past. Neither art, because its specialised skills are those of the craftsman, nor craft because it serves no evident utilitarian need, it belongs to the early Renaissance, before the division of the arts from the crafts. And if it escapes from the early Renaissance it is halted in the eighteenth century where it is subject to questions about its purpose; questions expecting specific answers about the occasion commemorated, the person portrayed, the presentation envisaged or the allegory elaborated; questions which in the eighteenth century could reasonably be asked about any work of art but which the nineteenth century myth of the artist as outcast and seer has taught us to regard as inappropriate to contemporary painting and sculpture. The answers too have lost some of their force. In the age of the photograph the power the portrait once possessed, as an icon embodying something of the spirit and power of the person portrayed, has been dissipated. In an age when history can be viewed on film the essentially static concept of commemoration seems dated and in an age which is habituated to the instant impact of advertisement the patience required to unravel allegory may be lacking (even if the artist continued to have access to a sufficient set of shared cultural norms to make its composition possible).

Yet this continuing closeness to tradition also has its strengths, since it is often the limits imposed by tradition that give medals their appeal, both to artists and to their public. Medals are small and small scale work has not been much in fashion in the arts since the Second World War. Both in sculpture and in painting the monumental has held sway. But it is possible that there is room for an art which, instead of competing with the sky-scraper and the expressway continues to relate to a human scale, as medals, which are made to be seen and appreciated while held in the human hand, are bound by their nature to do. Not that there is a necessary opposition between the large and the small. It may even be that the unintimidating nature of medallic work may result in greater sympathy towards and understanding of large scale sculpture; just as familiarity with large scale work and even blown up photos of the pieces themselves can help people to see medals more clearly.

Medals are multiples and multiples can create unease in a public used to the idea of the work of art as unique expression of the artist's feelings. But, like all multiples, they allow artists' work to be sold relatively cheaply, in a form which could be seen as the sculptural equivalent of the print, and so made available to a large number of people for enjoyment, not in the public and sometimes slightly chilly environment of a gallery or plaza, but in their own surroundings and whenever they choose.

Medal making is difficult. Modelling in low relief, engraving in steel and the use of lettering are skills which are no longer widely taught and which take time and effort to acquire. Both the processes of lost wax or sand casting, used for the majority of the pieces in this catalogue, and that of striking normally require access to expensive and elaborate equipment, entailing the use of a foundry or mint to carry out the stages between the creation of the model and the finishing and patination of the medals. But the challenge posed by these difficulties has its own attraction and the final result carries with it associations of durability that are central to the concept of commemoration and the, occasionally welcome, reverse of the intentional transience of some contemporary work.

The medallic format is restrictive. It is hard to compose within a circle and to create two images (obverse and reverse) which will compliment and strengthen each other while never, by the nature of the medal, being seen together. Yet the circle has its own fascination, carrying as it does connotations of the absolute that have given circular images a special place in every culture. And the two-sidedness of the medal, the relationship between inseparable images which can be seen in sequence, but never simultaneously, has inspired some of the most exciting pieces in this exhibition. What Ian Hamilton Finlay does in *Terror/Virtue*, Ron Dutton in *Pig Poem* or *Toilet Tangle*, Fred Rich in *Schools Curriculum Award* or Nicola Moss in *Cow-pat* could not be done in another medium.

The use of inscriptions has contributed to the medal's image as a pedantic and official medium. But in the work of Hamilton Finlay, as in Dutton's *Lightning* and his recent animal poems, inscription and image are fused so that the legend no longer acts simply as a description or explanation of the image but joins with it to form a single, unified work of art which transcends the division between sculpture and poem.

None of this is to claim that the artists in this exhibition have all become engrossed in the medallic tradition. But it is true that even the most apparently uncommitted artist may have shown a new aspect of their work through experimenting with the medal. Nigel Hall's *Bronze Shoal*, for example, is contained in a way quite uncharacteristic of his work, while at the same time liberated because it can be picked up and viewed from two sides and any angle, and Lynn Chadwick's *Diamond*

Ron Dutton
Pig Poem I 1985 (cat. no. 16)

makes explicit an opposition between male and female that may always have been present in his work but which has never been so succinctly expressed. It is also true that some of those who started very much on the periphery of the medallic tradition have been drawn by their exposure to it to an ever fuller exploration of the potential of the medal. If this exhibition communicates to its visitors even a part of the excitement of that exploration, it will have achieved its purpose.

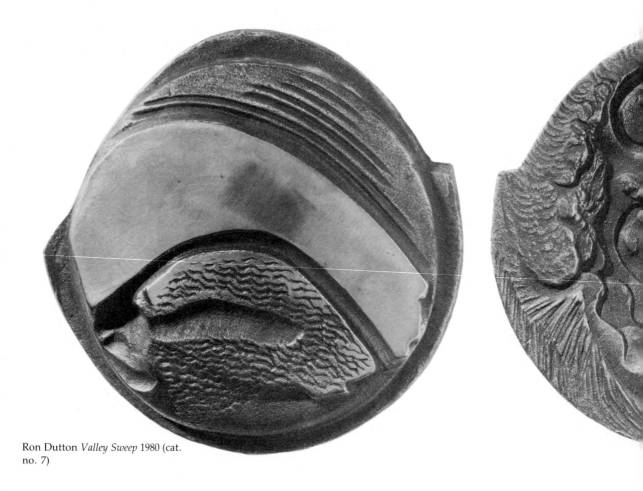

Ron Dutton *Valley Sweep* 1980 (cat.
no. 7)

The Catalogue

List of Artists

Malcolm Appleby

(b.1946)

Trained at the Central School of Art, the Royal College of Art and under John Wilkes, the well-known gunsmith. Himself one of Britain's leading gun engravers, Appleby's career as a medallist dates back to 1968 when he won first prize from the Goldsmiths' Company with his first attempt at die-sinking. Since then he has received a number of medallic commissions, from the Goldsmiths' Company, the Mammals Society and Collingwood Ltd (for the World Wildlife Fund).

Malcolm Appleby is unusual among contemporary medallists in directly engraving all the dies for his medals and in striking many of them at his studio in Crathes Station, Kincardineshire. This ties in with his belief that medals should be a normal part of everyday life, as demonstrated by his annual piece for the Crathes pantomime.

1 Human Butterfly 1973
Silver, 29 mm
Struck in an edition of 100, by the Royal Mint for the *Medals Today* exhibition, Goldsmiths' Hall, July 1973

2 Birds of Destiny 1973
Silver, 29 mm
Struck by the Royal Mint for the *Medals Today* exhibition. The birds represented are a rook and a stork

3 Owl 1973
Lead, 57 mm
A trial strike by the Royal Mint

4 Sun *c.* 1974
Silver, 22 mm
Struck by the artist

5 Loot 1976
Brass, 25.5 mm
Struck by the Royal Mint for the *Loot* exhibition, Goldsmiths' Hall, London and in Leeds, July and August 1976

6 Horrors of War 1983
Cast bronze, 42×20 mm
Inscribed beneath the base THE HORRORS OF WAR 1983, signed and numbered 13 (of an edition of 25).
The model was a group of melting plastic soldiers

7 Dick Whittington 1983
Silver, 22 mm
Struck by the artist for the Crathes pantomime. The legend reads HAS IT STARTED YET

8 Aladdin 1984
Silver, 21·5 mm
Struck by the artist for the Crathes pantomime
The legend reads WACK A DOO

9 Octopus/Turtle 1983
Cast gold, 31 mm
Made in an edition of 3

The pattern on the back of the turtle represents the Maze of Minos and that on the octopus a Nautilus Shell. The strands of the female octopus' reproductive organ become the skein of Ariadne as they enter the maze

6

1

2

3

4

5

7

8

9

Laurence Burt
(b. 1925)

Apprenticed to a firm of architectural metal workers at the age of fourteen. He studied part-time at Leeds College of Art (1949–55) and taught there and at Leicester College of Art, Cardiff College of Art, Wolverhampton Polytechnic, Hornsey College of Art and Falmouth School of Art.

He started exhibiting with the *London Group* in 1958 and has had one man exhibitions at the Drian Gallery, The Gallery, Falmouth and the Oriel Gallery, Cardiff. His work has also been shown at the Walker Art Gallery, Liverpool, the Tate Gallery, the Institute for Contemporary Arts, the Whitechapel Art Gallery and the Angela Flowers Gallery as well as in Germany and Cyprus. His work is in numerous public collections, including the Arts Council of Great Britain, the Tate Gallery, the Gulbenkian Collection, the Contemporary Arts Society of Wales, and the Muzeum Naradowe w Warzawie, Poland.

Laurence Burt now lives and works in York.

1 René Magritte 1983
Cast bronze, 77 mm
Cast by G. F. Lunt & Sons for the British Art Medal Society in an edition of 27

Michael Burton

(b. 1949)

Trained at Yeovil Technical College and the Sir John Cass School of Art, where he received a diploma (with distinction) in silversmithing.

His work has been exhibited in London, Bahrein, Tokyo, Melbourne, Basle, Chicago, Minneapolis and Leeds and is in the collections of the Victoria and Albert Museum, HM the Queen and the Goldsmiths' Company.

Michael Burton lives and works in Somerset.

1 Loot 1979
Bronze, 46·5 mm
Struck by the Royal Mint from hand engraved dies for the Goldsmiths' Company's 1979 *Loot* exhibition.

James Butler

(b. 1931)

Trained at Maidstone College of Art, St Martin's School of Art and the Royal College of Art. He worked as an architectural stone carver in the 1950s and as tutor of sculpture and drawing at the City and Guilds of London Art School (1960–75). His major commissions have included a statue of President Kenyatta for Nairobi (1974), a monument to the Freedom Fighters of Zambia for Lusaka (1973), of Richard III for Leicester (1980), and of Earl Alexander of Tunis for the Wellington Barracks, London. The portrait of Iris Murdoch shown here is his only medallic work.

James Butler is a Member of the Royal West of England Academy, Fellow of the Royal Society of British Sculptors and a Royal Academician (ARA 1964, RA 1972). He lives and works in a Victorian schoolhouse at Greenfield in Bedfordshire.

1 Iris Murdoch 1975
Struck bronze, 63 mm
Commissioned by the Food and Agriculture Organisation of the United Nations as one of its *Ceres* medals
Struck by the Royal Mint
(illus p. 12)

Lloyd Carter
(b. 1962)

Studied sculpture at Reigate School of Art (1979–84), where he is now a technical assistant. He has twice won bursaries in the Royal Society of Arts Medal Bursary Competition (1982, 1984) and has since received a number of medallic and sculptural commissions.

1 British Steel 1983
Cast bronze, 74 mm

2 Alfred Hitchcock 1983
Cast bronze, 69·5 mm
Won a bursary from the Royal Society
of Arts, 1984

3 Gala 1985
Cast bronze, 108·5 mm
Commissioned by the British Art
Medal Society

2

Lynn Chadwick
(b. 1914)

Worked as a draughtsman for various architects, including Rodney Thomas (1933–9 and 1944–6) and was a pilot in the Fleet Air Arm from 1941–4. In 1946 he moved to Gloucestershire and began producing designs for textiles and furniture. His mobiles were shown at Trades Exhibitions in 1947 and 1949 and in 1951 he was commissioned to make a number of pieces for the Festival of Britain. Exhibitions at Gimpel Fils and elsewhere were followed by a joint exhibition with Ivon Hitchens at the Venice Biennale in 1956 where he won the International Sculpture Prize. Since then his work has been shown in every major city in the Western world, including most recently (in the 1980s) Paris, Brussels, Toronto, Caracas, Montreal, New York, Edinburgh, Tokyo, Cannes, Chicago and Cologne. His most recent one man exhibition was at Marlborough Fine Art in 1984.

Lynn Chadwick's work is in a very large number of public collections, including the Tate Gallery, the Scottish National Gallery of Modern Art, the National Museum of Wales, the Musée Nationale de l'Art Moderne in Paris, the Galleria Nazionale d'Arte Moderna in Rome, the Kröller-Müller Museum in Otterlo, the Moderna Museet in Stockholm, the Museum of Modern Art in New York and the Hirschhorn Museum in Washington.

Lynn Chadwick lives and works at Lypiatt Park in Gloucestershire, where he has his own foundry. *Diamond*, which is thematically related to a large-scale work of the same name showing full length male and female figures, executed at the same time, is his only medallic work.

1 Diamond 1984
Struck bronze, 76 mm
Struck by the Pobjoy Mint for the
British Art Medal Society

Opposite *Diamond* 1984. Sculpture in bronze, Ht 198 cm

Geoffrey Clarke
(b. 1924)

After serving in the Air Force he studied at the Royal College of Art (1948–51) and shortly afterwards held his first exhibition, at the Gimpel Fils Gallery (1952). The wide range of his talents were amply demonstrated in his work for Coventry Cathedral which included stained glass windows, the high altar, a ten-foot high cross and candlesticks (cast in silver), a flying cross and crown of thorns.

Clarke has exhibited widely, both in one man exhibitions at the Redfern and Tranman Galleries, and in mixed exhibitions at the Royal Academy (he was elected ARA in 1970 and RA in 1976) and elsewhere and his work is represented in numerous public collections, including the Victoria and Albert Museum, the Tate Gallery and the Museum of Modern Art, New York. Other commissions have included an iron sculpture for the Time Life Building, New Bond Street, an aluminium relief for Castrol House, New Marylebone Road, mosaics for Liverpool University and Basildon New Town; a bronze sculpture for the Thorn Electric Building, St Martins Lane and many others in Britain and the United States.

Clarke's interest in medals was aroused both by their circular format, which he explored in his work in the late 1960s and by their potential as multiple and serial works. Four pairs of his medals, on the theme of Man's spoliation of the environment, were shown by Graham Hughes in his *Medals Today* exhibition in 1973. Following this, Clarke received commissions for medals for Tree Planting Year (for presentation by the Secretary of State for the Environment to those who had made outstanding contributions to the success of the campaign), Cowes Week, the Silver Jubiliee and the FAO.

Clarke's medals, unlike the rest of his work which is modelled in polystyrene and cast in aluminium, are usually modelled in plasticene and, for the most part, cast in brass by the artist. His earlier medals also depart from the mainstream in their use of a repertory of clearly representational images which have no direct relation to the abstracted forms employed in his sculptural work. Clarke's most recent medal, *Pyramus and Thisbe*, however, marks a new departure in his medallic work, being clearly related to recent large scale pieces, and modelled in much higher relief than had been employed in his earlier medals.

1

2

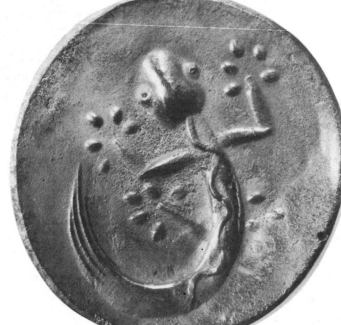

9

Three pairs of medals about the destruction of the environment.

1 Tree 1973
Brass, 46·5 mm

2 Stump 1973
Brass, 49 mm

3 Serpent in Tree 1973
Brass, 64·5 mm

4 Tree consumed by Serpent 1973
Brass, 63 mm

5 Full Container 1973
Brass, 64 mm

6 Spilt Container 1973
Brass, 64·5 mm

11

12

13

Wildlife medals

7 **Eagle** 1973
Brass, 85 mm

8 **Bee** 1973
Brass, 87 mm

9 **Gekko** 1973
Brass, 92 mm

10 **Lion** 1973
Brass, 96 mm

11 **Abbott** 1975
Aluminium, 115 mm

12 **The Sense of Smell** 1975
Lead, 50·5 mm

13 **Cowes Week** 1976
Zinc, 82 mm

14 **Silver Jubilee** 1977
Brass, 69·5 mm

15 **Pyramus and Thisbe** 1985
Bronze, 90 mm
Cast at Wolverhampton Polytechnic
    for the British Art Medal Society
Dedicated by the artist to Sam
    Wanamaker and the Globe Theatre

27

Gillian Colver
(b. 1961)

Studied at Canterbury College of Art, where she won a college scholarship, and the Central School of Art and Design where she won a Queen Mary's scholarship and received a first class honours degree. In 1984 she won a travel bursary in the Royal Society of Arts medal competition which she spent studying in Paris. She now works as a designer/jeweller at the South Bank Crafts Centre.

1 Shakespeare 1983
Bronze, 122×60 mm
Cast by G. F. Lunt and Sons
Intended as a prize medal for literature

Ron Dutton

(b. 1935)

Ron Dutton was born at Nantwich in Cheshire. He trained at Newcastle, in the Department of Fine Art, Kings College (later Newcastle University) and went on to teach sculpture at Wolverhampton Polytechnic from 1964–85.

Dutton's early work centred round the exploration of natural rhythms, both in performance art and abstract sculptures and it was not until the early 1970s, partly in response to a commission for a sports trophy, that he became interested in the potential of the medal. Since then, however, medallic art has been the keystone of Dutton's work and he has established himself as one of the most thoughtful and dedicated medallists alive today.

Although it was the sheer accessibility and functionality of sporting medals that initially attracted Dutton, his early work refers far more to his previous sculptural preoccupations than to the popular idea of the medal. In pieces like *Tree Rain*, elements of landscape are simplified into geometric forms which combine to produce compositions that rely for their effect as much on abstract and formal qualities as on any direct evocation of the subject. In the mid seventies, however, Dutton began to work direct from nature and, in works like *Little Rowan* and *Wave Breaks*, he conveys both an immediate impression of an element of landscape and a vivid record of the processes (scrape of palet knife, imprint of fingers in soft wax) that produce it.

The late seventies saw a break with certain elements of the medallic tradition, in particular the small scale circular format, and the exploration of others, including the relation between obverse and reverse in works like *Toilet Tangle* and *Sir Thomas Beecham*, and of the medallic series in *The Bathroom Suite*.

Building on this new direction Dutton returned to the exploration of landscape in groups of medals inspired by particular natural features, like Symonds Yat (*Wye Plough Edge, Valley Sweep*) and the Summer Isles (*Summer Isle Blue, Rock Lock*) in which two complementary elements of landscape experience appear on the two sides of a single work. Effects of weather are an essential element in such experience and in the early eighties Dutton returned to the single sided sketch format to produce a series of highly expressive representations of ephemeral effects, in which cloud and storm become as concrete and tangible as lake or hill.

At the same time as pursuing the essentially private and idiosyncratic goal of transmitting personal and ephemeral images of landscape into the immutable solidity of bronze, Dutton was also responding to a series of commissions. These enabled him to explore other aspects of the medallic tradition, among them the role of the inscription in terms of its contribution both to the overall composition and to the meaning of a medal. This experience has led, in his recent work, to an extension of the role of the inscription in a novel synthesis between image and inscription, which combine to create a new kind of three dimensional poem.

Ron Dutton's work has been shown in a number of one man exhibitions, most recently in the Tettenhall Gallery, Wolverhampton (1982, 84), Peter Dingley Gallery, Stratford-upon-Avon (1982), Keele University (1981), the Carlisle City Art Gallery (1980), the Ceolfrith Gallery, Sunderland (1980), the Usher Gallery, Lincoln (1977), the Hereford City Art Gallery (1976), the Oxford Gallery (1975) and the Wolverhampton Art Gallery (1975, 78). It has also been seen in exhibitions in Italy, Portugal, Sweden, Hungary and the United States.

Recent commissions have included coins for the Royal Mint and medals for the millennium of Wolverhampton, the centenary of the Fabian Society, the twenty-fifth anniversary of the Victorian Society and the tenth anniversary of Simpact Systems. His work is in numerous public collections in Britain, France, Holland, Norway, the United States, Hungary and Finland.

1 Tree Rain 1974
Cast bronze, 78·5 mm
Three in an edition of twenty

2 Little Rowan 1975
Cast bronze, 80 mm
One in an edition of twenty

1

3 **Wave Breaks** 1975
Cast bronze, 77·5×83·5 mm
One in an edition of twenty

4 **Toilet Tangle** 1978
Cast bronze, 74 mm
Part of the *Bathroom Suite*
One in an edition of fifty

5 **Sir Thomas Beecham** 1979
Cast bronze, 70 mm
Commissioned by B. A. Seaby Ltd
Nine in an edition of two hundred

6 **Wye Plough Edge** 1980
Cast bronze, 99 mm
One in an edition of sixty

7 **Valley Sweep** 1980
Cast bronze, 114 mm
One in an edition of sixty
(*illus* p. 18)

8 **Summer Isle Blue** 1980
Cast bronze, 85 mm
One in an edition of fifty

9 **Rock Lock** 1980
Cast bronze, 70 mm
One in an edition of fifty

10 **Aberdovey Pier light** 1982
Cast bronze, 91×109 mm
One in an edition of twenty

11 **Warnside Bottom Clump**
    1982
Cast bronze, 84 mm
Four in an edition of twenty

12 **Mr Thrower's Shropshire
    Garden** 1982
Cast bronze, 105×116·5 mm

13 **Plough Lines** 1982
Cast bronze, 100 mm
Two in an edition of twenty

14 **Sheep Storm** 1982
Cast bronze, 88·5×100 mm
Three in an edition of twenty

15 **Lightning** 1984
Cast bronze, 176×181 mm
The inscription reads LIGHT SPINNING
   JINGLING CLATTERING SPIKING
   SPITTING DOWN THE RHYMES OF FEAR
One in an edition of twenty

6

13

Robert Elderton
(b. 1948)

16 Pig Poem I 1985
Cast bronze, 78 mm
The inscription reads PRIM PRIME
   PORTLY PORKER POSING POSTURES
(illus p.17)

17 Sheep Poem I 1985
Cast bronze, 76 mm
The inscription reads SHEEP SHAGGY
   SHEEPISHLY STUMBLES SLIGHTLY
   STARES

Began a five year apprenticeship with the Royal Mint in 1964. During this period he spent a year full-time at the Central School of Art and later studied silversmithing at the Sir John Cass College of Arts. Since finishing his apprenticeship he has worked as an engraver at the Royal Mint designing and executing numerous coins, medals and seals, mainly for foreign governments.

He has been active as a medallist in private life and has completed numerous commissions including, most recently, a medal for the one hundred and fiftieth anniversary of the Royal Numismatic Society (1986).

Robert Elderton won first prize in the modelling section of the Goldsmiths' Crafts Council Competition in 1981 and in 1984 received the Best Senior Award for *Anna Pavlova*. His work has been exhibited at the Goldsmiths' Hall, the Royal Academy and in the exhibitions of the Royal Society of British Sculptors, of which he was elected an associate in 1981.

1 Beauty and the Beast 1972
Struck silver, 69 mm
One of four struck from dies directly
   engraved by the artist at the Royal
   Mint in 1972

2 John Lennon 1981
Cast bronze, 79 mm
The inscription beside the portrait
   reads IMAGINE, that around the
   bullet holes on the reverse SOMETIME
   IN NEW YORK CITY

3 Anna Pavlova 1983
Cast bronze, 90 mm

4 William Morris 1985
Cast bronze, 88 mm

14

1

2

Annabel Eley
(b. 1961)

Trained at Lincoln College of Art and at the Central School of Art, where she received First Class Honours in jewellery design in 1982. She has won a Queen Mary Award, the Royal Society of Arts Medal Bursary Competition and a recent competition for a medal to commemorate Christopher Blunt's eightieth birthday

Annabel Eley lives in London and has a workshop in the Portobello Road.

1 Thames Barrier 1982
Bronze, 84×61 mm
Cast by the Royal Mint
Winning entry in the RSA Medal
  Bursary Competition

2 Armour 1986
Bronze with silver inlay, 69 × 57·5 mm

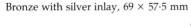

1

Ian Hamilton Finlay
(b. 1925)

Ian Hamilton Finlay was born in the Bahamas, went to school in Glasgow and briefly attended Glasgow School of Art before being called up in 1942. After the war he worked as a shepherd and agricultural labourer in the Orkneys, wrote short stories, plays and poems and moved to Edinburgh, where he founded the Wild Hawthorn Press (1961) and the periodical *Poor. Old. Tired. Horse.* (1962).

In 1963 *Rapel*, Finlay's first collection of concrete poems, was published soon to be followed by poem/cards, kinetic booklets, poem/prints and poems designed to be set in an environment. In 1966 Ian and Sue Finlay moved to Stonypath, an abandoned hillside croft, around which they were to create a famously beautiful classical garden.

The last issue of *Poor. Old. Tired. Horse.*, in 1968 was devoted entirely to poems, consisting of one word and a title. Finlay wrote 'It seemed obvious to me that one could not have a literally one-word poem on the page since any work must contain relationship!' In Finlay's later work this relationship was sometimes to be with an image (as in a medal or card) or with the surroundings of the poem (as in the garden at Stonypath).

In the 1970s there were major exhibitions of Finlay's work, at the Scottish National Gallery of Modern Art (1972) and the Serpentine Gallery (1977). This period also saw the emergence of his 'neoclassical rearmament project' and the beginning of a 'Five Year Hellenisation Plan' of the garden at Stonypath, now known as Little Sparta.

Finlay's first medals *Thunderbolt, Emden, Enterprise* and *Midway* are products of this period, concrete versions of the 'heroic emblems' which he published with Ron Costley and Stephen Bann in 1977. The relationship between medal and emblem in Finlay's work is particularly interesting because, as Michel Pastoureau has recently argued (in 'La naissance de la médaille' *Revue Numismatique* 1982) the medal, as a distinct art form, originates in the late medieval passion for devices or emblems, composed of a 'body' (image) and 'soul' (phrase), which found concrete form in the inscription and image that make up the reverse of a medal. Finlay's medals, unlike their now frequently impenetrable Renaissance predecessors, are accompanied by commentaries, written by Stephen Bann, which serve to clarify some aspects of the resonance of the medallic metaphor created by the combination of motto and image.

Recent years have seen conflict (the 'Little Spartan War') between Finlay and both the Scottish Arts Council and the Strathclyde Region, in the latter case over the status (for rateable purposes) of the Garden Temple at Little Sparta. *Flute* was issued to commemorate the First Battle of Little Sparta (1983), while *Terror/Virtue* is thematically related to the Intermediary Room in the Temple, which deals with Virtue, Terror and Revolution.

Ian Hamilton Finlay's international reputation has continued to grow, and 1985 saw his inclusion in the shortlist for the Turner Prize and the publication of *Ian Hamilton Finlay: A visual primer*, a major study of his work by Yves Abroux.

1

This series of four medals, and the silver version of the *Emden* were done in collaboration with Ron Costley. In each case the accompanying text is by Stephen Bann.

1 Thunderbolt 1975
Copper, 45×30 mm

Among the favourite subjects for the original *imprese* were the machines of contemporary warfare, siege-engines, flint-lock guns and numerous varieties of cannon. Finlay uses a modern equivalent of these citations from the technology of war. But he adds a 'motto' which alters the entire context of the device. The fragment quoted from the Pre-Socratic philosopher Heraclitus, implies that the tank's 'fire-power' is used here not simply as an index of its dominant role in modern field warfare but also to symbolize a cosmological scheme in which fire is the governing principle of the

universe. It is the modern equivalent of Heraclitus' 'thunderbolt', representing not only the supreme natural force of destruction, but also the dynamic element which regulates the natural world.

It is worth adding that this fragment from Heraclitus has attracted a number of interpretations. Part of the ambiguity resides in the fact that 'thunderbolt' is both a conventional personification of Zeus by synecdoche (part for the whole) and a metaphor pointing to the philosopher's own Cosmology. Finlay's *impresa* retains and transforms this ambiguity. The equivocal status of the tank suggests a conjuncture of traditional Epic form, in which the divine guarantee of order is always present, and the demythologised forms of Modernism.

2 Emden 1975
Copper, 45×28·5 mm

This medallion borrows the form of Finlay's earlier 'one-word poems', which created meaning from the conjunction of title ('Kleiner Kreuzer Sonata') and one-word text

('Emden'). The hinge of the poem is the identification of 'Kleiner Kreuzer' (Light Cruiser) and the famous 'Kreu(t)zer Sonata' for Violin and Piano by Beethoven. The classic status of the musical piece is also claimed for the exploits of the German warship *Emden*, which became a legend for its lonely forays against Allied shipping in the Indian Ocean at the outset of the First World War.

The nub of the poem is therefore a 'modern way with the classic'. Captain von Müller's achievement has been compared with that of the 'older French raiders' before the days of modern sea warfare, but his management of the 'detached ship' in modern conditions was at the same time brilliantly original. Connotations of virtuosity extend the basic parallel. Beethoven's sonata takes its name from the virtuoso to whom it was dedicated. Perhaps the elaborately devious course of the *Emden*, in the interval between its detachment from Admiral von Spee's squadron and its final sinking, can be seen as an unaccompanied cadenza for the virtuoso soloist.

3

4

5

6

7

3 Emden 1976
Silver, 74×47 mm

4 Midway 1975
Copper, 38 mm

Finlay's long-standing pre-occupation with the fishing-boat and its attendant imagery has within the last few years largely given place to a concern with the modern warship, and the panorama of recent sea warfare. Here he cites the Battle of Midway, which took place in June 1942 between the fleets of America and Japan and marked the turning of the Pacific war in America's favour. The motto picks up the famous opening lines of Dante's *Divine Comedy*: 'In the middle of the journey of our life ("Midway"), I came to myself in a dark wood'. The 'dark wood' of Dante's allegory is recreated in the bursts of anti-aircraft fire which cover the sky in surviving photographs of the Battle.

Earlier fishing-boat poems by Finlay had identified the 'steering' of the boat with the problems of choice in the moral world. This medallion uses the reference to Dante not simply to underline the conjunction of classic and modern, but also to amplify the element of moral allegory. This 'turning point' of the greatest naval war in history, as a result of which the aircraft carrier definitively supplanted the battleship, is an epic event. But once again it is an epic from which Zeus is as absent as is the promised theological outcome from the first lines of the *Divine Comedy*.

5 Enterprise 1975
Copper, 38 mm

The 'U.S.S. Enterprise' is not only a successor, in this series, to the Light Cruiser *Emden* and the Midway war fleets (the final, evolved exemplar of the modern warship), it also unites in itself the separate elements of the cosmology of Heraclitus. Earth is the landing ground offered by the carrier, air the element in which its aircraft move, fire its dynamic and destructive capacity and water the surrounding medium. Just as modern physics sets up a picture of the material world imaginatively analogous to that of the Pre-Socratic philosophers, so the nuclear-powered carrier embodies in an intimate and terrifying conjunction the power released by the splitting of the atom, and the poetic message of union of the elements.

Finlay's medallion can be seen in the context of the others in the series. But it also evokes a substantial group of works – poem-cards, sundials, and stone carvings installed around his home in Lanarkshire – that pursue the interwoven themes of Heraclitian cosmology and modern nuclear warfare. In his references to Pre-Socratic thought, Finlay places himself vicariously in the age just preceding that in which Western aesthetics have their origin. In his evocation of the modern fighting fleet, he bears witness to an age in which the epic view of warfare, the chivalric code and the romance of sea-faring have been decisively superseded. It is as if, by the operation of these two brackets (the first anticipating Platonic and Aristotelian aesthetics, and the second demarcating the codes of the past), the Western tradition has been placed in parenthesis. The self-contained form of the medallion is the precise correlative to this poetic act.

6 Terror/Virtue 1983
Bronze, 52·5 mm
Cast bronze by G. F. Lunt & Sons Ltd for the British Art Medal Society.

The accompanying text reads
THE GUILLOTINE represents (of course) Terror, the classical columns (a visual 'rhyme' borrowed from Puvis) not only Terror's reverse – here obverse – Jacobin Virtue, but the true Revolutionary mode

In the system of the French Revolution, what is immoral is politically unsound, what corrupts counter-revolutionary. Robespierre

There are besides, two little columnes or pillastres of this Throne; love appears on the right hand, and feare of Thy justice is to be seen on the left. Henry Hawkins

A republican government has virtue as its principle, or else terror. What do they want who want neither virtue nor terror? Saint-Just

Terror is the piety of the Revolution. Ian Hamilton Finlay

7 Flute 1983
Copper, 29·5×56 mm

The accompanying text reads
FIRST BATTLE OF LITTLE SPARTA
FEBRUARY 4, 1983

THE MACHINE-GUN is a visual pun (or play!) on Virgil's flute, with the vents in the barrel-sleeve as the finger-stops. But – *Et in Arcadia ego* – is the flute to begin, or the gun – or is the duet in fact to be a trio: does the singer (if he is to continue in his pastoral) need *both*?

Frank Forster

(b. 1952)

Trained at Middlesbrough Art College (1968–9) and at the City and Guilds of London Art School (1972–6), where he won the Beckworth Travelling Scholarship (1975) and first prizes for sculpture and drawing (1976).

Since then he has worked for Madame Tussauds (winning the Madame Tussauds Sculpture Prize 1976), the Faringdon Trust (a series of garden sculptures for Buscot Park), the Moyglare Stud (a bronze portrait of Habibti) and the Food and Agriculture Organisation (World Food Day Medal, 1983). Recently he has won a competition for an over life size statue of Clement Attlee which is to be sited in the new Mile End Park in the East End of London.

1 World Food Day 1983
Bronze, 50 mm
Struck by Picciani and Barlachi for the
   FAO

2 Michelangelo 1984
Bronze, 94 mm
Cast by the artist for the British Art
   Medal Society

2

Marian Fountain
(b. 1960)

Studied sculpture and design at the University of Auckland before coming to England on a Queen Elizabeth II Major Arts Council Travel Grant. She is now at the Scuola dell' Arte della Medaglia in Rome.

1 Woman 1983
Bronze, 54×65 mm

2 Monumenta 1985
Bronze, 68×40 mm
Cast, finished and patinated by the
  artist for the British Art Medal
  Society

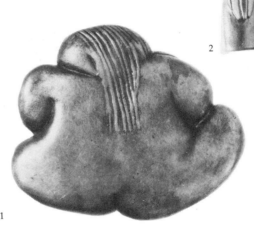

1

Elisabeth Frink
(b. 1930)

Studied at Guildford School of Art and at Chelsea School of Art under Bernard Meadows and Willi Soukop 1949–53. While still a student she exhibited at the Beaux Arts Gallery and with the London Group and her *Bird* was purchased by the Tate Gallery.

Since then Elisabeth Frink has become one of the best known and most admired of English sculptors. She has taught at the Chelsea School of Art (1953–61), at St Martins School of Art (1954–62) and at the Royal College of Art (1965–7). Major commissions have included the *Eagle* Lectern for Coventry Cathedral (1962), the Altar Cross for Liverpool Cathedral (1965), *Wild Boar* for Harlow New Town (1967), *Horse and Rider* for Trafalgar House (1974) and *The Dorset Martyrs* for Dorchester (1984–5). She has also illustrated *Aesop's Fables*, *The Canterbury Tales*, the *Odyssey* and the *Iliad* and executed portrait busts of Sir Alec Guinness (1983), Lord Richardson (1984) and Sir Georg Solti (1984), and many others.

Elisabeth Frink's medals, though peripheral to her work as a sculptor, reflect both her preoccupation with the strength and grace of her animal subjects and, in the case of the MIT medal, with the reduction of man's inhumanity to man. Their tactile forms are also typical of her work and suggest a direct and enthusiastic involvement with her materials. In the Bison the forms have been built up to a crusty finish, suggestive of a bovine sturdiness, while in the MIT medal, the message of Universal Peace has been created by the grace of the incised line across the globed form.

Elisabeth Frink is a Royal Academician (ARA 1971, RA 1977) and a Dame of the British Empire (CBE 1969, DBE 1982).

1 Bison 1975
Bronze, 76×83 mm

Commissioned by Lord Zuckermann, on behalf of the Zoological Society of London, for presentation to eminent British zoologists. The funds came from the Federation of British Zoologists, which had been wound up in the 1960s

Presented by the artist

2 Peace Medal 1977
Silver, 69×86 mm

Commissioned by Lord Zuckermann on behalf of the Massachusetts Institute of Technology for presentation to the givers of a series of lectures on World Change and World Security

Presented by the artist
(illus p. 5)

1

2

Nigel Hall

(b. 1943)

Trained at the West of England College of Art, Bristol (1960–4) and the Royal College of Art (1964–7) before taking up a Harkness Fellowship (1967–9).

Recent one man exhibitions have included shows at the Juda Rowan Gallery, London, the Galerij 565, Aalst, the Galerie Nicole Gonet, Lausanne, the Galerie Klaus Lüpke, Frankfurt, the Nishimura Gallery, Tokyo and the Galerie Reckermann, Cologne. His work is in numerous public collections, including those of the Arts Council, the Art Institute of Chicago, the Australian National Gallery, the Museum of Modern Art, New York, the Musée Nationale d'Art Moderne, Paris, the Nationalgalerie, Berlin, the National Museum of Art, Osaka, and the Tate Gallery.

1 Bronze Shoal 1982

Bronze, 79 mm
Cast by G. F. Lunt and Sons Ltd for the British Art Medal Society in an edition of twenty-one

The group of works to which this medal belongs (which includes both drawings and sculptures) were inspired by the movement of shoals of fish, hundreds of individuals turning as one. The word shoal also conjures up the image of sandbanks in shallow water, the former image being appropriate to the medal when vertical, the latter when horizontal

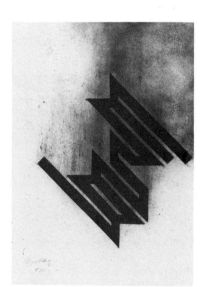

Drawing no. 235 1981. Charcoal on paper, 75·7 × 56·6. Courtesy Juda Rowan Gallery. Photo: George Meyrick

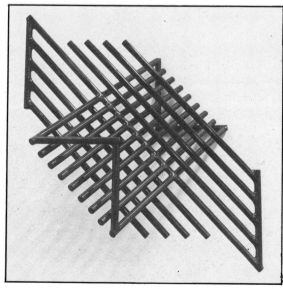

Alternative (to Silence) 1981. Painted aluminium, 48·3 × 6 × 29 cm. Coll. Nicola Jacobs. Photo: George Meyrick

Mark Holloway
(b. 1956)

Studied at Reigate School of Art and Design (1974–8) before working as a studio assistant to Enzo Plazzotta, Robert Glenn and Geraldine Knight. In 1975 he won the Royal Society of Arts Medal Bursary and since then he has executed medallic portraits of Herbert Seaby (for BA Seaby Ltd) and Elizabeth Fry (for Bedford College).

Mark Holloway now lives and works in the south of Spain.

1 Muse 1982
Bronze, 70×50 mm
Cast by G. F. Lunt and Sons Ltd for
   the British Art Medal Society in
   an edition of twelve

Jonah Jones
(b. 1919)

Studied at the King Edward School of Art, Newcastle, before doing national service in the 224 Parachute Field Ambulance and Educational Corps (1940–6). After having worked in the Eric Gill Workshops he set up on his own in Gwynedd in 1951.

Since then he has been a member of the National Council for Diplomas in Art and Design (1961–71) and Chairman of its Fine Art Panel (1968–71), Director of the National College of Art and Design, Dublin (1974–8), a lecturer at Newcastle University (1980–1) and Arts Fellow of the University of Wales (1981–2). He is at present Chairman of the Mostyn Gallery in Llandudno.

Jonah Jones' work has been widely exhibited and he has received a number of commissions for stained glass, sculpture and inscriptions. In 1981 he executed the Dylan Thomas plaque for Westminster Abbey and he has done numerous portrait busts, including John Cowper Powys, Bertrand Russell, Sir Huw Weldon, and Sir Clough Williams Ellis.

1 Dylan Thomas 1975
Bronze, 125 mm
Cast in sand by Hogans for the British
   Art Medal Society
The reverse inscription reads DYLAN
   THOMAS 1914–1953, and in the
   centre *Time held me green and dying*

Rod Kelly
(b. 1956)

Trained at Birmingham Polytechnic and at the Royal College of Art, in the Department of Silversmithing (MA 1983). His work is in a number of public collections, including the Victoria and Albert Museum, and he has recently received commissions from the Goldsmiths Company, Mecca and the Grosvenor House Antique Fair.

Rod Kelly lives in London and has a workshop in Old Street, north of the City.

1 Schumacker Medal 1983
Silver, 51×69 mm
Commissioned by the Intermediate
  Technology Development Group
  for presentation to outstanding
  ecologists

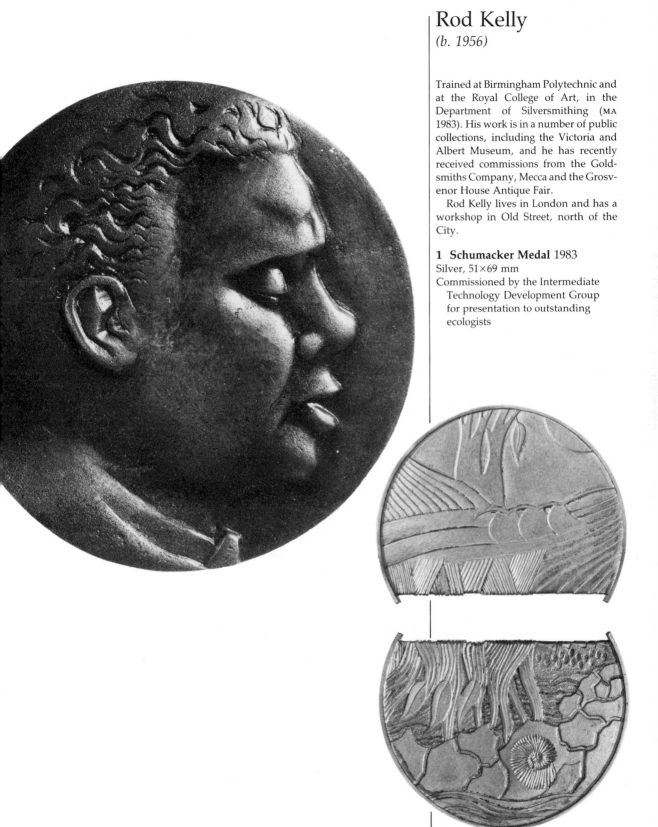

Fred Kormis

(b. 1897)

Born in Frankfurt where, at the age of fourteen, he was indentured as an apprentice in a workshop specialising in the production of decorative sculpture and mouldings. In 1914 he won a scholarship to the Frankfurt Art School, but the following year he was conscripted into the Austrian army, sent to the Eastern front, wounded and captured. In a Siberian prison camp he modelled medallic portraits of his fellow inmates in clay until, in 1920, he escaped and returned to Frankfurt. There a successful career as a portrait sculptor and medallist was ended by Hitler's advent to power. Kormis moved, first to Holland and then to London where he exhibited at the Beaux-Arts gallery and estab-

lished a studio in Sherif Road. In 1940 this was hit by a bomb and all his large scale work destroyed. Partly as a result of this upheaval the war saw a renewed concentration by Kormis on medallic work. His famous portraits of the War Cabinet and of the distinguished exiles then gathered in London were produced at the same time as an extensive series of medallions for the Jewish Museum in New York.

Since the war Kormis has returned to large scale sculpture, but he has also continued to produce occasional portraits of contemporaries, modelled from life, which together make up one of the most distinguished portrait galleries of our time.

1 Sir Michael Tippett 1977
Bronze, 131 mm
Cast by Morris Singer Ltd in an
edition of four

2 Menachem Begin 1978
Bronze, 135 mm
Cast by Morris Singer Ltd in an
edition of eight

3 J. B. Priestley 1978
Bronze, 132 mm
Cast by Morris Singer Ltd in an
edition of three

4 John Schlesinger 1983
Bronze, 113 mm
Cast by G. F. Lunt and Sons Ltd for
the British Art Medal Society in
an edition of eighteen
(*illus* p. 6)

1

Cecilia Leete
(b. 1961)

Jane McAdam
(b. 1958)

Trained at Brighton Polytechnic and the Central School of Art and Design where she received a first class honours degree in three-dimensional design. In 1983 she won first prize in the De Beers' Diamonds Today competition and a travel bursary in the Royal Society of Arts medal competition (spent in Egypt, the Sudan and Kenya). In 1984 she was commissioned to produce one of the prizes for the Schools Curriculum award.

She lives and works in a newly founded group of craft workshops off London Fields in East London.

1 Winter Olympics 1982
Bronze, 50×95 mm
Cast by the Royal Mint
A winning entry for the RSA Medal
   Bursary Competition of 1982–3
(*illus* p.14)

2 Theatre 1983
Bronze, 76×58 mm
Cast by G. F. Lunt and Sons Ltd for
   the British Art Medal Society in
   an edition of twenty-four
Finished and patinated by the artist

3 Schools Curriculum Award
   1984
Bronze, 74·5 mm
Cast by Hector Miller
Twenty silver examples were made of
   which eighteen were awarded to
   winning schools

Studied art at the Wimbledon School of Art (1976–7), mosaics in Ravenna (1977–78) and jewellery design at the Central School of Art and Design (1978–81) before doing post graduate work at Goldsmiths' College (1981–2).

Her Picasso medal won first prize in the 1981 Royal Society of Arts Medal competition and since then she has executed a number of medallic commissions, including ones for the Schools Curriculum Award (1984), and Morgan Grenfell (1984). Her work has recently been exhibited in the FIDEM exhibitions at Florence (1983) and Stockholm (1985), in the *Young Blood* exhibition at the Barbican (1983) and in the Oxford Gallery. With the assistance of an award from the Prince's Trust she established a workshop in Brick Lane, in the East End of London, and now sells her jewellery regularly from a stall in Greenwich.

1 Picasso 1980
Bronze, 90×80 mm
Cast by the Royal Mint for the Royal
   Society of Arts medal competition,
   in which it won an award
An edition of twenty-seven was later
   produced by the British Art
   Medal Society (1982–3)
(*illus* p. 13)

2 The School and the
   Community 1984
Bronze, 71×71 mm
Cast by Hector Miller for the Schools
   Curriculum Awards
Nineteen silver examples were made
   of which seventeen were
   awarded to winning schools

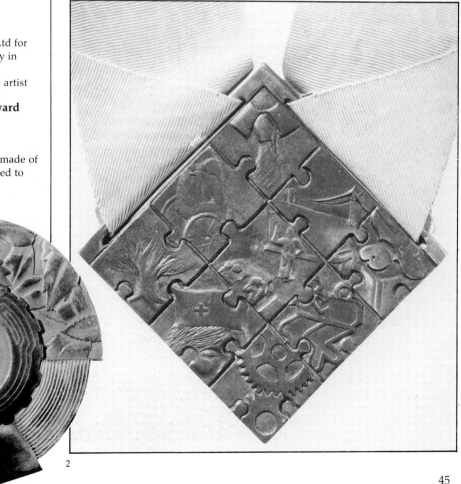

3

2

John Maine
(b. 1942)

John Maine was born in Bristol and studied there, at the West of England College of Art (1960–4) and then at the Royal College of Art in London (1964–7), where he won the Walter Neurath Prize (1966) and the RCA Drawing Prize (1967). From 1967–9 he held a fellowship at the Gloucestershire College of Art and Design, returning to London to set up a studio in Shoreditch in 1970.

In 1972 John Maine had his first one-man exhibition, at the Serpentine Gallery. He also began to show his work regularly in group exhibitions, including *Steel Sculpture* (Mappin Art Gallery, Sheffield, 1972), *The Condition of Sculpture* (Hayward Gallery, 1975), the *Silver Jubilee Exhibition of British Sculpture* (Battersea Park, 1977), Cleveland International Drawing Biennale (1977, 1979, 1981), the *British Art Show* (Sheffield, Newcastle and Bristol), the Hayward Annual (1982) and the *Sculpture Show* (Hayward Gallery, 1983).

In 1979–80 Maine was a fellow at the Yorkshire Sculpture Park; in 1980 he worked near Carrara in Italy; in 1981 at Hagi in Japan and in 1983–4 in Australia, carving granite. More recently he has completed a large sculpture on the South Bank of the Thames in front of the National Theatre. Entitled *Arena*, this consists of a twisting ring of closely interlocked stones. The form emerges from ground level, giving the impression that its geometric structure could continue in a mirror image below the pavement. There are breaks in the circle forming entrances, and opening up various cross sections of the ring.

Turning Circle developed out of the intricate geometry of ellipses in Maine's earlier work, but certain characteristics of *Arena* can also be detected in this medal. Both convey a sense of curving motion, and each, in its own way, interrupts this continuity.

Southern Ellipse 1980. Carrara marble, 1·98 × 1·98 × 1·40 m. Sun Life Court, Bristol

Model for *Arena* 1983

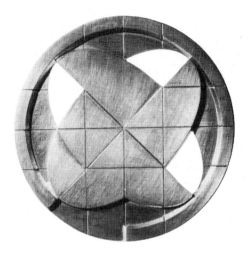

1 Turning Circle 1983

Silver, 60 mm

Struck by Thomas Fattorini in an edition of thirty-eight bronze and ten silver, each of which was finished and patinated by the artist

About this medal John Maine has written:

After several drawings the original model was made in wood 172 mm diameter. The procedure was similar to engineering pattern making, where for example wooden prototypes are made for wheel castings.

The form was reduced mechanically, and dies were cut in metal. Lead versions of the medal were struck before the dies were hardened, to see how it was developing and to allow minor changes to be made. It was important to follow each stage of the work in order to respond to changes of scale and material.

The medal was approached as a small sculpture. While working elsewhere on large stone pieces, it was a contrast to consider an object which could be encompassed by the hand. Although its elliptical structure had been the basis of earlier

carvings such as *Prism* (1977), *Turning Stone* (1978) and *Southern Ellipse* (1980), it would have been pointless to make a miniature version of an existing idea. A new approach was needed to explore the possibilities of the relief within a circle.

The medal's basic geometry is described by various incised lines. It is pierced in three places and these holes define the volume and act as references between the two faces, creating a unified form rather than two reliefs placed back to back, as is more usual with medals.

Nicola Moss
(b. 1960)

Studied at Hertfordshire College of Art
and Design and at Canterbury College
of Art where she did a degree in sculpture. In 1984 she won a scholarship to
the International Medallic Workshop
held at Pennsylvania State University.

Nicola Moss is now working at the
Bristol Sculpture Shed, both on large
scale sculptures and on medals.

1 Cow-pat 1984
Bronze, 100 mm

Both this and the following medal
were cast at the International
Medallic Art Workshop held at
Pennsylvania State University in
Summer 1984

In this piece she opposes the dream
to the reality of country life

2 Heads and Tails 1984
Bronze, 66 mm

1

Philip Nathan
(b. 1941)

Trained at Guildford School of Art (1957–62), where he specialised in carving and terracotta modelling and then at the Royal Academy Schools where he won the silver medal for sculpture. He then worked for the Royal Mint as an engraver/designer (1965–8) and at the Franklin Mint (1968–73) where he produced numerous coins and medals including a set of thirty-eight pieces for the Royal Shakespeare Company. Since 1973 his free-lance work has included designs for the first national coinage of Barbados, medals for the Queen Mother's eightieth birthday, the Westminster Medallion for the House of Commons, the Royal Wedding crown and a series of medals for Operation Raleigh.

Philip Nathan is a fellow of the Royal Society of British Sculptors (ARBS 1966, FRBS 1978) and recently received the American Numismatic Association's gold medal for excellence in the field of numismatic art.

1 John Paul II 1982
Bronze, 55 mm
Cast for Spink and Son Ltd to
commemorate the visit of the
Pope to England

Paul Neagu
(b. 1938)

Paul Neagu was born in Bucharest and studied at the Institute of Fine Art there (1959–65). His early work included performance, paintings, drawings, stage designs and tapestries. In March 1969 his work was shown at the Richard Demarco Gallery in Edinburgh and late in 1970 he moved to London (becoming a British citizen in 1976). In the early 70s he taught at Queen's University, Belfast, and Hornsey College of Art, conducted *inquests* on Titian, Cranach and Brancusi, and showed his sculpture at the Serpentine Gallery.

The foundation of the fictitious 'Generative Art Group' in 1972 presaged the appearance of the hyphen, or generator in his work in 1975. Neagu's hyphens serve a sculptural function equivalent to that of the grammatical hyphen which acts both to link and to separate words. At their simplest they are formed from an oblong supported on legs, the pointed ends of which form a triangle and which, rotating, inscribe first a circle then, as they continue, a spiral. These forms, ascending in complexity from the triangle, whose three points are the minimum needed to enclose space, through the oblong to the circle which opens out into a spiral, are also invested with symbolic and even metaphysical significance.

The hyphen, with all its ramifications in a growing family of related forms, has been central to Neagu's work of the last ten years and has been seen at the Institute of Contemporary Arts, the Whitechapel Gallery, the Air Gallery, the Laing Gallery, the Sunderland Art Centre and the Third Eye Centre in Glasgow, as well as in the United States, France, Japan and Switzerland. It is the tenth anniversary of its presence in his art that was celebrated by Neagu in his first medal in 1985.

1 Ten Years of Hyphen 1985
Bronze, 100 mm
Cast for the British Art Medal Society

Paul Neagu wrote the following about
   this medal:
Sculpture's history is marked in all
periods and cultures, along
centuries, with 'hyphens' . . . that
particular moment of mediation
between time and space, between
energy and matter, a link as a
neutral referent of anchoring.
Hyphen is a pivot and a pointer.
The Greeks called a 'herm', a plinth
with a phallus on which a guiding
and guarding head was placed as
catalyst for the traveller. I have
made many hyphens, of many
materials, since 1975. My own
interpretation is embedded in the
symbolic geometry of sculptural
articulation which combines
metaphor with concrete palpable
texture. The medal I made in 1985 is a
celebration of this awareness; on its
own a double faced seal which wants
to mark the constancy of
relationship and betweenness.

Martin Page
(b. 1952)

Martin Page trained at the Central School of Art (1970–3) and the Royal College of Art (1973–6). He has exhibited at the Electrum Gallery and at the Goldsmiths Hall and was commissioned by the Goldsmiths to produce medals for their 650th anniversary and for a number of *Loot* Exhibitions, in the late 1970s. He has also received medallic commissions from the Royal Statistical Society, and the Paintmakers Association.

Martin Page is a part-time lecturer at Plymouth School of Art and lives in Cornwall.

1 Loot 1978
Bronze, 44·5 mm
Struck by the Tower Mint from
    directly engraved dies
Reverse: the Gera Gallery in Jaffa

Ronald Pennell
(b. 1935)

Trained at Moseley School of Art and Birmingham College of Art. Internationally known as a glass and gem engraver, his work has been exhibited in numerous international exhibitions and he won the second prize in Fragile Art International, San Diego, USA (1982). He also won the West Midlands Arts Prize in 1976 and his work has recently been seen at a one man exhibition at the Oxford Gallery. His work is represented in numerous public collections including those of the Corning Museum, New York, the Crafts Council and the Czechoslovakian State Collection.

Ronald Pennell lives and works near Hoarwithy in the Wye Valley.

1 'Good Growers' Gardening Medal 1976
Silver, 40·5 mm
Struck from dies hand engraved by the artist

2 Landscape 1980
Silver, 41·5 mm
Struck from a die hand engraved by the artist

3 Hedgehog by Moonlight 1980
Silver, 41 mm
Struck from a die hand engraved by the artist

4 A Tree for Me 1984
Bronze, 50 mm
Obverse: engraved on a glass lens, from which moulds were taken and a medal cast in silver
Reverse: carved on the silver medal which then served as a master from which moulds were taken for the bronze examples

About this medal the artist wrote:
A tree for me shows a man wheeling away the last ancient tree in a **wheelbarrow perhaps for preservation in a museum!** The serpent, with all it represents in mythology and christianity, observes all. On the reverse, three dead trees in a barren landscape. I am an optimist, but everyone alive today must think from time to time – where, when and how will it all end?

1

2

3

4

Carl Plackman
(b. 1943)

Born in Yorkshire. After studying architecture and mathematics he turned to sculpture, first in Bristol and then at the Royal College of Art (1967–70), where he won the Walter Neurath Drawing Prize and the Sculpture Drawing Prize. His numerous exhibitions have included one man shows at the Felicity Samuel Gallery, the Arnolfini Gallery, Bristol and the Chapter Arts Centre, Cardiff, and a recent exhibition (1984) at the Studio Odd in Hiroshima.

Carl Plackman now lives in London and teaches at the Goldsmiths' College of Art. His work is represented in a number of public collections, including the Victoria and Albert Museum, the National Museum of Wales and the Henry Moore Centre at the Leeds Art Gallery.

1 Reason versus Pleasure 1984
Bronze, 108 mm
Cast by G. F. Lunt and Sons Ltd for
  the British Art Medal Society.

Of this medal the artist wrote:
It can be said that one of the major problems to beset both personal and social development since the establishment of Greek culture has been the conflict between reason and pleasure.

Reason attempts to rationalise performance.
It acts as a constraint for imagination and pleasure and the discovery of the self.
Those who pursue reason are rewarded.
Those who pursue pleasure are condemned.
These principles are seen very much in positive and negative terms.
This conflict is very apparent in the different ideologies and actions exemplified in the miners' strike [of 1985].

The overall shape of the medal is in the form of a divided millstone. The basic necessity (bread – which is processed by the 'stone') is struggled for, and held, on the one hand by the negative shape of a sledge-hammer, and on the other prised up by the positive form of the pickaxe. These 'tools of the trade' can

be seen as allegories for basic attitudes towards 'work' and the principles or purposes we attach to it. The ambiguity of the ball and chain/balloon above the negative sledge-hammer is like the choice of perspective we may attach to this

activity. Is it to be celebrated or condemned? (Above the pickaxe on the left several echoes of this shape can be seen reflected in a negative form). The cord leading from this sphere is transformed into the concentric circles on the surface of the millstone. These lines could be expanding from the centre or shrinking into it. A millstone not only grinds things down it 'refines' them. It both destroys and re-creates and has become one of the common emblems in the conflict which arises in the pursuit of reason and pleasure.

Peter Quinn

(b. 1943)

Educated in Egypt, Germany and Singapore. Worked as a press photographer before studying at Brighton College of Art (1961–4) and the Royal Academy (1965–8).

Peter Quinn lectures in sculpture at Reigate School of Art and Design. He specialises in privately commissioned portrait work, mainly for American clients. He has exhibited at the Royal Academy and his work is in the collections of the Manchester City Art Gallery, the Greater London Council, the Trades Union Congress and London University.

1 John Betjeman 1984
Bronze, 105 mm
Cast by G. F. Lunt and Sons Ltd for the British Art Medal Society.
Finished and patinated by the artist

Fred Rich
(b. 1954)

Fred Rich trained at the Central School of Art (1977–81). Thrice winner of Goddards awards for design in silver (1979, 1980, 1982), he came first in the Royal Society of Arts medal bursary competition (1981) and was awarded a first class honours degree in jewellery (1981).

His medallic work is remarkable both for its use of colour, in the form of enamel, gold and platinum leaf and ribbons, and for the skill and wit with which obverse is related to reverse. Recent commissions include the Schools Curriculum Award Medal for the Society of Education Officers and the Biochemical Research Medal for the Wellcome Trust, a badge of office for the Goldsmiths' Company and a necklace for De Beers.

Fred Rich lives in London. He teaches jewellery and medal making at the Central School and has a workshop in Portobello Green.

1

1 Osprey 1983
Gilt and enamelled bronze,
   66×57·5 mm
Commissioned by the British Art
   Medal Society
Cast by G. F. Lunt and Sons Ltd in an
   edition of sixty

**2 Schools Curriculum Award
   Medal** 1984
Gilt and enamelled bronze, 65 mm
Cast by Hector Miller
Twenty five examples were made in
   silver of which twenty three were
   awarded to participating schools

**3 Wellcome Trust Medal for
   Research in Biochemistry
   related to Medicine** 1986
Bronze, 80×75 mm

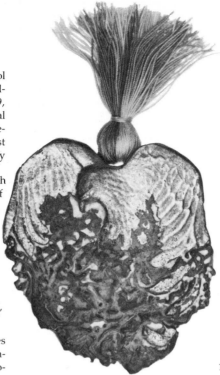

2

Michael Rizzello
(b. 1926)

After military service (1944–7) in India and the Far East he studied at the Royal College of Art (1947–50) and, after winning the Rome Prize for sculpture, in Rome (1951–3).

His public commissions have included the National Memorial to David Lloyd George (Cardiff) and official medals for the nine-hundredth anniversary of Westminster Abbey (1965), the Investiture of the Prince of Wales (1969) and the Churchill Centenary Trust (1974). He has also designed coinage for over ninety countries.

Michael Rizzello is President of the Royal Society of British Sculptors, a past president of the Society of Portrait Sculptors and a Fellow of the Society of Industrial Artists and Designers.

1 Dolphin 1984
Bronze, 90 mm
Cast by G. F. Lunt and Sons Ltd for the British Art Medal Society in an edition of sixty five

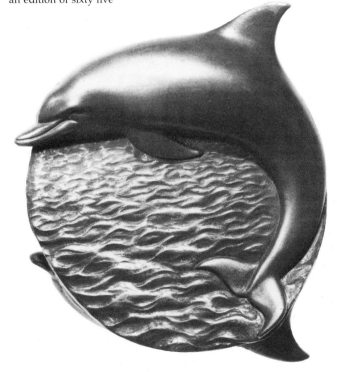

Ivor Roberts-Jones
(b. 1913)

Trained at the Goldsmiths' College Art School and the Royal Academy Schools. Served in the Royal Artillery (1939–46). Taught sculpture at the Goldsmiths' College School of Art (1946–68). His work has been seen in one man exhibitions at the Beaux-Arts Gallery (1957), the Oriel Gallery, Cardiff (1978) and the Eisteddfod (1983) and numerous group exhibitions. His public commissions include Winston Churchill (Parliament Square) and Attlee (Members Lobby, House of Commons) and his sitters have included Somerset Maugham, Yehudi Menuhin, the Duke of Edinburgh, Geraint Evans and Viscount Tonypandy.

Ivor Roberts-Jones' work is in numerous public collections, including the Tate Gallery, the National Portrait Gallery, the National Museum of Wales and the Arts Council of Great Britain.

1 Kathleen Kenyon 1975
Bronze, 63 mm
Struck by the Royal Mint for the FAO

Ronald Searle
(b. 1920)

Ronald Searle was born in Cambridge and it was in the Cambridge Evening News that he published his first cartoons in 1935. From 1935 he worked at the Co-op, attending Cambridge School of Art part time until in 1938 when he won a scholarship and became a full time art student.

The following year he joined the Royal Engineers and was employed exploding landmines and constructing pill boxes until transferred to a Camouflage unit in 1940. Sent to the Far East at the end of 1941 he was captured by the Japanese in February 1942 and sent to work on the Thai – Burma Railway, after which he spent the remainder of his captivity in Changi prison, in Singapore. His experiences during the period are recorded in a number of drawings which have recently (1986) been shown at a major exhibition in the Imperial War Museum.

On his return to England after the war, Searle moved to London where he enjoyed increasing success with his St Trinians drawings, illustrated numerous books, designed films and worked for *Life* magazine.

Though enormously successful he grew disenchanted and in 1961 abandoned everything and left for Paris. There he continued to work on films, including *Those Magnificent Men in their Flying Machines*, *Homage to Toulouse-Lautrec*, *Scrooge* and *Dick Deadeye*, contributed to the *New Yorker* and travelled widely as a pictorial reporter. He also began, at the suggestion of Pierre Dehaye, then Director of the Paris Mint, to make medals. Starting with a brilliant self portrait in 1973, which showed the artist, about to be laureated by 'La Gloire', he went on to do a medallic history of caricature. His early portraits in this series – of Carracci, Ghezzi, Hogarth, Gillray, Rowlandson and Cruikshank – mainly done in 1974 – were struck from dies, engraved after drawings, but in 1975 he modelled a medal of Edward Lear and by 1977 he was producing magnificently powerful and fluently modelled medals of Posada, Dix, Grosz and Thurber.

Searle's work has been widely published and seen in numerous exhibitions, including major retrospectives at the Bibliothèque Nationale, Paris (1973) and the Staatliche Museum Preussischer Kulturbesitz, Berlin (1976). His medals and models for medals have recently (1986) been shown at the British Museum.

Since 1978 Ronald Searle and his wife Monica have lived and worked in a hill village in Provence.

1 Self-portrait 1973
Bronze, 72 mm
Struck by the Paris Mint in 1975
Made from dies engraved after
    drawings by the artist in 1974
Reverse: *La Gloire* kneels on the flat
    plain of Searle's native land
    (Cambridge), ready to crown him
    with a laurel wreath

2 Jose Guadalupe Posada 1977
Copper, 68 mm
Struck by the Paris Mint in 1981
Made from dies reduced from models
    in 1977

3 Otto Dix 1977
Bronze, 68 mm
Obverse: from a self-portrait
Reverse: from a water-colour by Dix
Struck by the Paris Mint in 1981
Made from dies reduced from models
    made in 1977

4 George Grosz, 1977
Copper, 68 mm
Reverse: after Grosz's drawing *Circé*
    for his book *Das Neue Gesicht der
    Herrschenden Klasse* in which the
    profiteer is transformed into a pig
    by the goddess he embraces

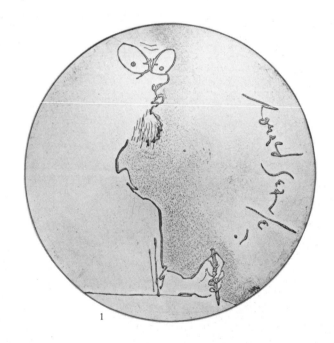

1

5 James Thurber 1977
Bronze, 68 mm
Struck by the Paris Mint in 1981
Made from dies executed in 1979 after
    models made in 1977
Obverse: taken from a drawing by
    Searle of Thurber, done in 1958
    when the latter had lost his sight
Reverse: from *The Seal in the Bedroom*
    (1932)

6 Tim Bobbin 1978
Bronze, 68 mm
Struck by the Paris Mint in 1981
Made from dies made in 1980 after
    models dating from 1978
Obverse: a portrait of Bobbin, after
    engravings by Sanders and Hogarth
Reverse: taken from Bobbin's
    Human Passions Delineated (1773)

7 Charles Dickens 1983
Bronze, 71 mm
Struck by the Birmingham Mint for
    the British Art Medal Society in 1984
Made from models completed in 1983

8 Samuel Pepys 1984
Bronze, 71 mm
Struck by the Birmingham Mint for
    the British Art Medal Society in 1985
Made from models completed in 1984

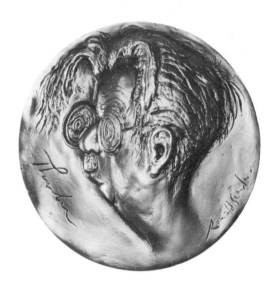

5

7

Jacqueline Stieger
(b. 1936)

Studied at Edinburgh College of Art (1952–8) where she won the Royal Scottish Academy Award (1957). In 1965 she had a one-woman exhibition in the Galerie Reihentor, Basle, and moved to Switzerland where she lived from 1966–69.

Jacqueline Stieger's first medals were exhibited at the *Medals Today* exhibition in 1973 and in the following year her *Grow Food* won the *Prix Renouveau de la Médaille*. Numerous medallic commissions since then have included three medals for the Goldsmiths' Company, a portrait of Barbara Ward for the FAO, a medal for the 1981 conference of the British Association for the Advancement of Science, the McKechnie Lecture Gold Medal for Liverpool University and the Arms and Armour Society Medal. Her sculpture, jewellery and medals have been seen in numerous exhibitions in Britain, North America and Europe. Her most recent one-woman exhibitions have been at the Galerie Reihentor (1983) and at the Copernican Connection, Beverley, (Autumn 1985).

Jacqueline Stieger lives and works near Brough, in Humberside, where she casts and patinates almost all her own work.

1 **Grow Food** 1974
Bronze, 69·5 mm
Cast by the French Mint
Five in an edition of fifty

2 **Harrogate Festival** 1975
Silver, 83 mm
Commissioned by the Goldsmiths'
  Company
Cast by the artist
(illus p. 11)

3 **Goldsmiths' Hall, Jaffa** 1978
Bronze, 81·5 mm
Commissioned by the Goldmiths'
  Company
Cast by the artist

3

4 British Association for the Advancement of Science 1981
Bronze, 49·5 mm
For the 150th anniversary meeting at York
Cast by the artist

5 Arms and Armour Society 1983
Bronze, 47 mm
Commissioned by the Society for presentation to individuals who have made an outstanding contribution to the study of the subject
Cast by the artist

6 Diploma Design Award 1984
Bronze, 74×86 mm on a base 170×140 mm
Commissioned by the School of Architecture, Humberside College of Education
Cast by the artist

7 William Kent 1985
Bronze, 54·5×63 mm
Cast by the artist

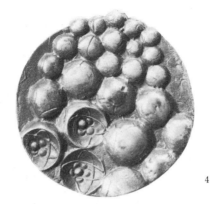

4

6

7

Joan Thompson
(b. 1943)

Trained at Brighton School of Art (1960–4), the Royal Academy Schools (1964–6), where she won the Landseer Prize and silver medal (1965, 1966), the British Institute Award (gold medal, 1966) and the Edward Stott Travelling Scholarship, and the Royal Society of British Sculptors (1966–7).

Since then she has been Head of Sculpture at the Sir John Cass School of Art (1967–3), has restored antique sculpture in wood and ivory and done designs for the Royal Court theatre and Glyndebourne Opera House.

Joan Thompson's work has been exhibited in London, Montreal, New York and Jaffa. At present she is working mainly as an ivory carver and portrait sculptor.

1 **Papageno/Papagena** 1985
Bronze, 79 mm
Cast by RED Bronze

2 **Pisces** 1985
Bronze, 69 mm
Cast by RED Bronze for the British Art Medal Society

2

Paul Vincze
(b. 1907)

Trained at the School of Arts and Crafts in Budapest and under Ede Telcs. He travelled to Rome on a scholarship (1935–7) and came to England in 1938, taking British nationality in 1948.

His numerous medals include Yehudi Menuhin's 50th birthday medal (1966), the Shakespeare-Garrick medal (1969), a medal for J. B. Priestley's 80th birthday (1974), and the International Shakespeare Association Congress medal (1976). He has also designed coins for Libya, Guatemala, Ghana, Guernsey, Nigeria, Guinea, Malawi, Uganda and Jamaica. He has exhibited at the Royal Academy and at numerous international exhibitions and his work is represented in the Museum of Fine Arts, Budapest, the Ashmolean Museum, Oxford, the Swedish Historical Museum, the Danish National Museum, the Smithsonian Institution, Washington, and the Cabinet des Médailles, Paris.

Vincze has been awarded a *Premio Especial* at the International Exhibition, Madrid (1951), a silver medal at the Paris Salon (1964) and the gold medal of the American Numismatic Association. He is a Fellow of the Royal Society of British Sculptors.

1 **Bicentenary of Browne & Co** 1975 (reverse)
Bronze, 56 mm

2 **Self Portrait** 1977
Bronze 56 mm

2

George Weil

(b. 1938)

George Weil studied at St Martins School of Art and at the Central School (1956–61). He started companies producing jewellery and objets d'art in the late 1950s and has exhibited widely in Britain, Belgium, Switzerland, Israel, the USA and Japan.

Three medals from a series of six in memory of the Holocaust

1 Bound Figure 1984
Bronze, 87 mm

2 Six Candles 1984
Bronze, 88 mm

3 Appeal for Help 1984
Bronze, 87 mm

4 St George 1985
Bronze, 98 mm

4

3

David Wynne
(b. 1926)

Educated at Trinity College, Cambridge and served in the Royal Navy (1944–7). Though lacking any formal art training he became a sculptor in 1949 and was soon exhibiting work at the Leicester Galleries (1955, 1959), Tooth's Gallery (1964, 1966) and the Findlay Galleries, New York (1967, 1970, 1973). Since then his distinctive public sculpture has become familiar throughout Britain and the United States and he has been commissioned to do portrait busts of a great number of distinguished contemporaries. David Wynne also designed the fifty pence piece for Britain's entry to the European Community and the Queen's Silver Jubilee Medal (1977).

1 Olave Baden-Powell 1973
Bronze, 63 mm
Struck by the Royal Mint for the FAO

Wynne modelled a bust of Lord Baden-Powell in 1971

Brief Glossary of Technical Terms

CASTING
(See *Lost Wax Casting* and *Sand Casting*.

DIE
The medal design is cut into this. It is normally cylindrical and made of steel which is hardened, by the application of heat, after the steel has been *engraved*. It may also be made of iron or bronze.

EDITION
The number of copies of any medal produced. The size of an edition will depend both on public demand and on the process used to produce it. Casting involves low fixed costs (the moulds) but is very labour intensive. Cast medals therefore tend to be produced in editions of 2–100. Since steel dies are expensive to produce, striking involves a higher initial outlay than casting. However struck medals are quick to make and require little finishing, so large numbers can be produced at a low unit cost (as many as 100,000 examples of a struck medal have been produced).

ENGRAVING
Cutting the required image into a *die*. This process can be done manually or by a machine (see *reducing machine*) and is also referred to as *die-sinking*.

FINISHING
Working on the medals to remove the imperfections left by the casting process.

LOST WAX CASTING
Moulds are taken from the artist's model. Wax is poured into the moulds, making wax replicas of the model. The waxes are then invested (packed) in fire resistant material. The investment is heated so that the wax runs out and a space, the size and shape of the model, is left into which molten metal is poured.

MINT
An organisation which strikes medals or coins.

MODEL
The artists original model may be made in a variety of materials, including wax, plasticene, clay, plaster and wood. It is often produced in two stages; after the artist has modelled the overall design in relief he/she takes a plaster impression from the relief model and engraves details, including the inscription in intaglio.

PATINATION
Colouring metal, normally by the application of chemicals and heat.

REDUCING MACHINE
A three dimensional pantograph that enables dies to be produced directly from large relief models (*c.* 25 cm). The best reducing machines were made by a French company called Janvier & Cie.

SAND CASTING
The artist's model is used to impress images of each side of the medal in two boxes of cohesive sand. The boxes are then brought together, leaving a space the size and shape of the model which is filled with molten metal.

SPLASH STRIKING
The pressure applied by the press used for striking causes the metal of the blank to spread. To prevent this the blank is normally contained in a collar. Where no collar is used the process is described as splash striking.

STRIKING
Producing medals by placing a blank piece of metal between two dies and applying sufficient pressure to the upper die to force the metal to take the imprint of the design from both dies. This process places great strain on the dies so, unlike cast medals which can be of any size or shape, struck medals must be relatively small (normally less than 100 mm in diameter) and a fairly low relief (not more than 10%).

Further Reading

Lynn Chadwick – Recent Sculpture Exhibition catalogue, Marlborough Gallery, 1984.

Ron Dutton's Medallions Exhibition catalogue, Ceolfrith Gallery, Sunderland, 1980.

Yves Abroux *Ian Hamilton Finlay – A visual primer* Reaktion Books, Edinburgh, 1985.

Elisabeth Frink Exhibition catalogue, Royal Academy, 1985.

Nigel Hall – Recent Sculpture and Drawing Exhibition catalogue, Juda Rowan Gallery, 1985.

Paul Neagu – Sculpture Exhibition catalogue, Institute of Contemporary Art, 1979.

Ronald Searle in Perspective New English Library, 1984.

The Art of the Medal Mark Jones, British Museum Publications, 1979.

Médailles Periodical, 1937–

The Medal Periodical, 1983–